Gifts of Transition and Healing

Gifts of Transition and Healing

Mary Ellen Barton

Copyright © 2010 by Mary Ellen Barton.

Library of Congress Control Number:	2010915763
ISBN: Hardcover	978-1-4568-0119-9
Softcover	978-1-4568-0118-2
Ebook	978-1-4568-0120-5

All rights reserved. No part of this book may be reproduced or transmitted in any form or by any means, electronic or mechanical, including photocopying, recording, or by any information storage and retrieval system, without permission in writing from the copyright owner.

This book was printed in the United States of America.

To order additional copies of this book, contact:
Xlibris Corporation
1-888-795-4274
www.Xlibris.com
Orders@Xlibris.com

Contents

Introduction	9
Dad's Story	11
Brad's Story	14
Kevin's Story	17
Jim's Story	20
Nancy's Story	26
Wedding Story	29
Mom's Story	32
Elma's Story	37
Jane's Story	40
Intuition	44
Rory's Story	46
Matthew's Story	49
My Personal Angel	55

To Nigel

Thank you for all of your love, commitment, and support.

All of my love,
Mary Ellen

Introduction

My life, thus far, has been an interesting journey. Since a very early age, death has been very much a part of my life. My favorite cousin died suddenly when I was ten. My father died the following summer. Since then I have lost two brothers, my mother, my in-laws, and many friends.

As an adult, I was first a nurse working in children's intensive care and then managing newborn intensive care and labor and delivery. My nursing career then evolved into both hospice care and AIDS care, finally spending the last eight years, again, in children's services. I was blessed to spend the last years of my nursing career helping to further develop children's hospice care in Scotland.

Because of this, the dying process has been a very integral part of my life. Although there is much grief in this, I have come to also see all of the gifts in being allowed to be a part of people's lives at this crucial time. Each experience has provided me with much learning and many, many gifts.

One of these gifts is the experience of both giving and receiving Reiki. Reiki is an ancient Eastern technique of channeling the universal life force or, simply put, 'healing energy'.

Over the last few years, I have felt compelled to acknowledge at least a few of my experiences of transition and/or healing and share them with others.

Thus the title, *The Gifts of Transition and Healing*.

Symptoms of Inner Peace

A tendency to think and act spontaneously
Rather than on fears based on past experience.

An unmistakable ability to enjoy each
And every moment
To its full expression
Regardless of whatever others may think of it.

A loss of interest in interpreting
The actions of others.
A loss of interest in conflict,
Sarcasm, or any kind of abuse.

A loss of the need for worry or fear.

Frequent outbursts and episodes of
Overwhelming ecstasy and appreciation
For people and life.

Feelings of contentment and connection
With others and nature.
Frequent attacks of smiling
Just for the fun of it.

An increasing tendency to surrender
To the way things are
Rather than forcing them to happen
Out of their due time.
An increasing susceptibility to the love
Extended by others
As well as an uncontrollable urge to share it
A sincere desire to make this world
A better place to live
Because of your hope for peace,
Love and prosperity for all.

Author Unknown
But greatly appreciated

Dad's Story

My father was forty-three when I was born. I had two brothers, nineteen and twenty years old, and they were what we referred to in the 1940s as a 'second family'. My father had been a heavy smoker, but after having two heart attacks in his late thirties, he had quit. When I came along, he told people that he felt he had been given a second lease in life and that I was 'his' girl. We did just about everything together.

One summer evening in June, when I was eleven, he took my younger sister (yes, they had another one!) and I to Dairy Queen for an ice-cream cone. When we came back outside and got into the car, he turned to me with a very sad, serious look on his face. He told me that he would soon be going to heaven. He said that he was going there to build a home for my mother and us girls. He told me not to be afraid and that he would still be with me and look out for me. Lastly, he asked me to look out for myself and the rest of the family, as I was the strong one. This all seemed very confusing and overwhelming, but I took it as a fact because he was my dad.

Two weeks later, the parish priest, who was a very close friend of my father, pulled up in our driveway in the middle of the morning. I immediately knew that he had come to tell us that my father had died. Dad had collapsed over his desk at work while telling some of his staff a joke. He made his transition laughing, which was very much the way he would have wanted to go.

The following few years were very hard. My mother's grief and depression only grew, and she ended up in a psychiatric hospital several times. I did feel that I was the one to keep the family together, very much assuming the parent role.

At age thirteen, things were very hard at home. My mother had begun dating a man with schizophrenia, and home had become very chaotic and sometimes dangerous.

One evening, as I was going to bed, I sat down on the side of my bed. As I looked toward my bedroom door, I saw my father standing there. He was surrounded by a blue light. He didn't say anything out loud. He just stood there smiling at me for what seemed a very long time. It was as if he was telling me the things I needed to know without speaking. Things like 'be strong', 'I'm here for you and you are safe', 'do what you know is the right thing regardless of what anyone else says'. From that day forward, whenever I had to make a decision about handling a difficult situation, I would ask myself what Dad would do and follow that course.

I always wondered if it was my imagination and never told anyone about that special night.

I grew up and became a nurse. I was always pulled to care for people dealing with their own mortality. When I was in my forties, I was doing AIDS and hospice work. A very close friend had recently died and I was feeling very sad. Another friend and mentor of mine suggested that I could use a fun day out and that I should go with her to a lecture at a nearby medical center. It was to be about dream interpretation, and she thought it would be interesting and helpful to both of us.

The speaker was a doctor of psychology, who had done extensive work in this area. At the end of the day, she left a time for questions. After several questions, someone asked her if our loved ones really do come to us in our dreams, and if they do, how do we know when it is really them and when it is just a dream or our imagination.

After a moment, she stated that she usually didn't go into these areas, as all people didn't believe in an afterlife. She then said that the studies regarding this seem to have several things in common. One was that when it was really the person who had made their transition, they had a blue light around them. Another was that they didn't speak but seemed to give you the information you needed through thoughts.

I was very excited about this, so when I went to visit my mother the next day, I told her about my experience when I was young and what the lecturer had shared. She became very solemn and asked me again how old I was when this happened. She then said that she had also seen my father about the same time and that he also had a blue light and 'spoke' with her the same way. She had never told anyone because it had scared her.

For the first time, my mother and I began talking about spirituality. Our relationship grew deeper than I had ever thought possible.

To this day, I look to my father for guidance when making decisions.

Brad's Story

It was the late eighties and I had just moved to Alabama. My company transferred me there in order to establish a new location. I was a nurse for a home-infusion company. We administered intravenous pain control, antibiotics, chemotherapy, etc., to people who wished to receive these treatments at home rather than at the hospital and were stable enough to do so. One of our specialties was AIDS care.

My first call was to provide pain control for an AIDS patient, who was at the end stage of his illness and wished to be home with his sister and her family. When I arrived, I first met his sister, who was his main caregiver. She was very well versed in his needs and very anxious to do all she could to make Brad's last days comfortable.

Brad was too weak to speak but still had a beautiful smile and said much through his eyes and expressions. I did what I could over the next few days to support them. His sister, Nicole, and I quickly became friends.

After Brad's death, Nicole and I stayed in touch. We began getting together for lunch on a regular basis. We were each at a stage in our lives where we were looking at our own spirituality and life purpose—her because she had lost her brother and best friend, me because I was working with so many very ill and/or terminally ill people.

One Saturday morning, several months after Brad's death, Nicole showed up at my front door. This wasn't unusual. What was unusual was that she had her arms full of things I didn't recognize and appeared very angry. I invited her in and asked what was going on. She explained that Brad had come to her in her daily meditations and told her that she must give me Brad's bedspread and one of his vases. The bedspread was a beautiful silk spread. I was actually getting ready to buy a new one, as my kids had just visited from university and confiscated mine. All she knew about the clay vase was that he collected clay art, and this was one of his favorites. She told me that he was very definite and that I was to take them quickly before she changed her mind. I knew that Nicole found it very difficult to give up anything that had belonged to Brad, so I felt very sad about accepting these things.

Since that time, I always had treasured both of these gifts. I always felt very safe sleeping under the bedspread and kept the clay vase displayed proudly.

Four or five years had passed, and I was at a Native American art display. I was surprised to see a vase shaped exactly like the one Brad and Nicole had given me with almost the same design on it. When I asked about it, the artist told me that they were called spirit pots and that some Native Americans keep these after a loved one has died. They believe that the vase houses the spirit of their loved one. He explained that it was about honoring the loved ones, who had gone to the Great Spirit. The vase now had much more importance for me.

Eight years after moving to Alabama, I found myself again moving. This time it was to Scotland! I had fallen in love with a wonderful British man, and he had asked me to move there and marry him.

After several months of searching for the right job, I found myself working at the Children's Hospital in Edinburgh. It was my responsibility to coordinate home care for children with complex needs.

One of my first patients was a beautiful little girl named Allie, who had AIDS. Her mother had already died of AIDS. She and her father were very close, and both were determined that she would stay at home for the remainder of her life. I was blessed to have a few months to get to know Allie and her family. Everyone commented on how Allie seemed to be a wise old soul. The nurses and doctors said several times that when Allie looked at you, it was as if she could see right inside of you. Maybe it was because she had already been through so much. On one of my visits, she mentioned that she was always very cold. The first thing that came into my mind was Brad's bedspread. I asked her if she would like a special bedspread that would keep her very warm. She didn't say much but I got one of her few smiles and her eyes lit up. The next day, I took the bedspread to her. She loved it. Her dad later told me that she said it made her feel like a princess. He told me that when other kids came around, she wouldn't let them touch it. This was unusual, as Allie was very kind and shared whatever she had. She would tell her friends that this bedspread was meant just for her, to keep her warm and safe.

Allie kept this bedspread with her for the rest of her all-too-short life. When she died, her family asked if I would mind if they buried her with the bedspread, as Allie had made this request. Only then did I realize that I had only been a messenger / delivery person from Brad to Allie. Everything had happened in perfect order. I now feel that Brad must have been there to help Allie through this ordeal.

Kevin's Story

I had become good friends with Kevin and John while working with an HIV support group. I was coordinating care for AIDS clients. Sadly, Kevin then became one of my clients. One of my responsibilities was to be on call for emergencies.

It was a sunny, summer Saturday afternoon, when I received a call from John. He told me that Kevin was in the emergency room at the local hospital and that the doctors had said that there was no more that they could do for him. Kevin had slipped into a coma earlier in the day, and he was dying.

I hurried to the hospital. John was with him and wanted to know what he could do for Kevin. Kevin had a lot of tubes and wires, and John was a little scared to disrupt anything. I suggested that he ignore the tubes and wires and hold Kevin, talk to him, and assure him that he, John, would be all right. I encouraged him to let Kevin know that it was safe to move forward towards the light. As John did this, I watched Kevin take his last breath. It seemed that I could feel his spirit leaving and the grey room becoming lighter. I then noticed that John wasn't looking at Kevin but up at the ceiling above Kevin, reaching towards something and mouthing 'good-bye'. He then turned to me and said, 'Did you see that? Did you see Kevin leave?' Up until this time, John had always stated that he had no spiritual beliefs and didn't think there was an afterlife.

For the next two weeks, I did what I could to support John through the funeral and other arrangements that had to be made.

At this time, I was also in the process of changing jobs. On this particular day, my present boss phoned me to say that he would be coming to town the next day to pick up my company car. This shouldn't have come as a surprise, but things had been very busy, and I hadn't thought yet about getting another car.

The next evening, John showed up at my door. I invited him in, thinking that he wanted to talk. (He knew nothing about my job change.) He said, 'No, I'm actually in a hurry and the car's running'. Confused, I then asked, 'Why are you here?' He proceeded to explain to me that he had been wondering what to do about Kevin's car. He couldn't afford two car payments, and it was painful to think about selling it. John then explained that Kevin had come to him in a dream the previous night and said, 'Don't you get it? Mary Ellen's suppose to get the car!' Kevin had only made his transition two weeks ago, and he was already looking out for me. What a blessing!

The Seed

The seed that is to grow
Must lose itself as seed;
And they that creep
May graduate through
Chrysalis to wings.

Wilt thou then, O mortal,
Cling to husks which
Falsely seem to you
The self?

—Wu Ming Fu, Chinese poet and philosopher

Jim's Story

I don't know where to start with this story. For reasons I'll never completely understand, losing Jim was one of the hardest things I've ever experienced. I guess I'll start at the beginning.

When I moved south to set up home-infusion therapies for a national company, I soon became immersed in HIV/AIDS care. I often felt inadequate to give the proper support to those dealing with AIDS and knew I needed to learn more—and quickly. To this end, I joined the AIDS Coalition, and before I knew it, I was acting as their coordinator of direct services. That meant finding resources for care, where there often weren't any.

One of the first people I met was Jim. He had a face that lit up with a beautiful smile whenever he greeted anyone. He cared very deeply about serving this population but was determined not to let life get him down. He managed to see the positive, light side of situations. He was the treasurer for the coalition, which meant we spoke most days, putting our heads together to figure out where and how to find funding to help our clients.

He also had AIDS and frequently had side effects or secondary infections, but he never complained. He was always too focused on others and how he could serve them. People loved being around him because he could make them laugh. They knew how much he cared. I never knew Jim to judge anyone.

For many of us, Jim was the one that was going to make it. He was going to beat the odds. So when Jim became very ill and then quickly terminal, I walked around in disbelief. His partner, many of his closest friends, and I spent every minute that we could at the hospital. Jim was still very alert but had a general neuropathy. This resulted in him being too weak to talk. It also caused him much pain when he was touched. So much of our time was spent just sitting quietly with him.

On this Saturday afternoon, Jim's partner, Bill, and I were standing by the bedside. Bill was telling me that Jim's and his biggest regret was that they had not had a spiritual blessing of their union. They had planned for one at the end of the month. Jim had even had the invitations made and was about to send them out when he became ill. As if on cue, their minister walked into the room. I left Bill and the minister to have a conversation but came back into the room just as she was leaving. As she walked out of the room, I suddenly had a thought and was compelled to act on it immediately. I hurried out of the room and caught up with the minister. I told her of Jim and Bill's sadness about not having this spiritual union and asked her if there was anything that could be done on such short notice. We both knew Jim's death was imminent. She thought for a minute and then said that there was no reason that it couldn't happen that day. We went back to the room and ran it by Jim and Bill. Bill was delighted. You could see by the smile on his face that Jim was also.

Bill and I began phoning their close friends, and within minutes, they began to arrive. We all gathered around Jim's bed, and the minister performed the most beautiful 'wedding' I had ever attended. We were all in tears, except Jim. He was smiling from ear to ear! As she finished their blessing, Jim looked at Bill and mouthed, 'I love you'. These were the first words Jim had said in days, and his last.

We all continued to gather around Jim's bed for the rest of the evening. Jim's breathing was becoming irregular and shallow, and we all knew Jim was soon to leave us.

It was now midnight and we were all weary. Nothing had changed for hours, and we couldn't believe how Jim just kept going. He seemed to be barely there. Bill held Jim several times and told him that it was okay to let go, to go forward to somewhere where he would again be whole, pain-free, and happy. Still he held on.

We were now sitting on the floor in a circle around his bed and sharing wonderful, funny stories about Jim. It was seven minutes after midnight. We were all laughing at a 'Jim Story'. We looked up and Jim took his last breath. We were all very sad, but also, each felt a sense of complete peace come over the room.

Slowly, we all left the hospital to try to get some sleep. We all agreed to meet later in the day to begin to plan Jim's memorial.

That morning, I was standing in front of my bathroom mirror, unable to think at all, trying to get ready for the day. Suddenly I heard Jim's voice very clearly saying, 'Silly, I wasn't going to die on my wedding day!' I realized immediately that that was the answer to why Jim had held on so long. And of course, Jim would choose to go when laughter was filling the room. I jumped in my car and drove over to Bill's home. When he answered the door (at 7:30 a.m.), he looked at me as if I were crazy. When I told him the reason I had come to see him so early in the morning, he knew for sure that I was. But I knew it was Jim's voice! I was too numb and tired to think of anything on my own that morning. And to this day I can hear how clear his voice was. After hearing about it, everyone's response was, 'Of course, Jim would do that!'

The next day, Bill asked me if I would go to the funeral home with him. He and Jim's family were going to meet with the mortician. He was very anxious because Jim had left very specific requests about what he wanted done. Their favorite place to go was a lake on the Tennessee River. Jim had asked to be cremated and his ashes spread on the lake. Jim's family had very different ideas. They had been in the same town for generations and had family plots. It was very important to them that Jim be buried with the rest of the family.

As I sat in the mortician's office with Bill and Jim's family, I had a feeling of great sadness and helplessness. But about fifteen minutes into the discussion, I had a thought and felt compelled to speak up. I looked at the mortician and asked, 'Since Jim wished to be cremated, is there any reason why all the ashes have to be kept together?'

After recovering from shock, the mortician thought for a moment and then slowly said, 'No, I guess not'. So Jim had the funeral and burial that his family needed in order to deal with their grief; and Jim's partner and friends had a day out on the lake, telling stories about Jim, crying and laughing and scattering his ashes.

I frequently felt Jim's presence and guidance when working with other AIDS clients and was glad I had a special angel I could call on for help.

I thought that this was the end of this story, but after writing it, I now feel compelled to continue and tell you what I experienced over the next few months.

During this time, one of my friends suggested that I go with her to a seminar about dreams that was being offered at a nearby university medical center. (This is the same seminar that I refer to in 'Dad's Story'.) There were about fifty people at this seminar, and it seemed an interesting but uneventful day until the last hour. At that time, the professor opened the session for questions. Someone asked, 'If a loved one who has died comes to you in your sleep, how do you know if it's a dream or if they are really there?' She stated that it was her experience that if they were truly there, you saw them face on, and they had a blue light around them. This had happened to me when I was twelve, a year after my father died. This felt very affirming to me. Another person then asked if she believed in life after death and whether we could really make contact with our loved ones. She said that she was now not speaking for the university but for herself and her own experiences and that she usually didn't discuss any of this in her classes. She went on to say that besides being a doctor of psychology, she was clairvoyant. She then said that she was saying this because she sometimes channeled those who had died and that someone was now connecting with her and insisting on giving someone in the class a message. By this time, we were all sitting in stunned silence! She then pointed to me (in the back of the room) and said she had a message for me from Jim but that I already knew he was connecting and that I had been feeling his presence and getting messages from him. While I sat there with my mouth open, she said that Jim had some messages for me, and she would like to meet with me after the seminar ended. I agreed.

I met with the speaker, and she led me to her office. She sat down, said Jim was there, and began speaking to me with names and terms Jim often used when talking with me. She said she knew that Jim had died of AIDS and that he wanted me to know that even though I worked with the virus daily, I would never contract this disease. At this time, there was still much to know about the virus. He said that they wouldn't find a cure for some time yet but that, in the meantime, I would be helping to control the pain and symptoms. This would not just be the traditional care I now helped to give but that I would be healing with my hands. I didn't have a clue about what he was speaking. He also said that the cure would eventually be from the root of a plant that grows in the desert.

He continued to say that he knew that I had been very sad but that soon I would be very happy. That I would be given a choice about whether I wanted to stay on earth and that if I chose to stay, I would have much love and happiness and be moving across the 'big pond'. He also gave me some very specific financial information that prevented me from having what could have been a financial disaster.

About three months after Jim's death, I was referred by my doctor for a mammogram. This was just part of a routine physical that was required for my employment. The day after my mammogram, I received a call from my doctor, who asked me to come in to discuss my tests. It appeared that I had a breast tumor, six inches deep and directly over my heart. My first thought was, 'Grief does strange things!' I had a biopsy and it was cancer. During the time since Jim's death, I had begun searching for answers and looking at my spiritual beliefs—again. I had just started meditation classes. During my class the week of this diagnosis, I decided to ask Spirit for some answers. So during meditation, I asked what I needed to do in order to regain my health. Immediately, I was given the words visualization, Reiki, and nutrition. I knew what visualization and nutrition were about, but I had never heard of Reiki. (This was in 1992.) So after class, I asked my instructor if he knew anything about it. He said he didn't understand it, but someone had just leased a room in our building to do massage and Reiki. He then said that he thought she was there at the moment and took me to meet her. She seemed a bit taken aback when I asked her for a treatment. She was just setting up her room and didn't have music or anything yet. She asked me if I knew what it was, and I replied, 'No. But I've been guided to have it so here I am'. She said she would do a treatment, and then she would explain it and answer my questions.

As I lay on the table with my eyes closed, she put her hands on the top of my head. When she did this, I 'saw' liquid golden angels flowing through my head and down through my body. For the rest of the treatment, I lay there peacefully, just relaxing. After the treatment, she asked me if I felt anything during the treatment. I started to say that I had just felt very peaceful but then remembered what I experienced at the beginning of the session. She said, 'At the beginning? When I had my hands on your head?' I answered, 'Yes'. And she explained that that was when she prayed and asked the angels to assist with the healing. I confirmed that they were definitely there! I continued my Reiki treatments, along with nutritional changes and visualization.

The doctors couldn't seem to decide what type of treatment and surgery was needed (lumpectomy, mastectomy, etc.), so I asked my surgeon if I could do things my way for a while. We agreed that I would have a mammogram each month. If the tumor was growing, I would have surgery. Each month, the tumor was smaller, and in six months, it was gone.

After my recovery, I decided that I wanted to learn Reiki so I could do it for myself and others. It's a method of channeling healing energy to someone for the purpose of healing. It's done by placing your hands on them and allowing the energy to flow. Since that time, I've learned the three levels of Reiki and became a teacher.

A year after Jim's death, I met someone and fell in love. He asked me to marry him and move to Scotland. You can imagine my surprise when he asked me to 'move across the big pond!'

Besides working as a nursing manager while in Scotland, I began teaching Reiki. I was blessed to teach Reiki to many nurses and parents caring for children with long-term illnesses or special needs. They found this very helpful in controlling pain and other symptoms.

It's now fifteen years later, I've moved back to the States, and am more happily married than ever. I'm approaching the big '6-0' and am looking forward to another exciting, blessed stage of my life. Knowing that we are eternal beings and that death is merely a door we walk through on this forever journey helps me to appreciate each day. I no longer have any fear of death, which enables me to live. I realize that it's all a blessing; it's all lessons to help us on our path as spirits, who have chosen to walk this earth path for the present moment.

I thank Jim every day for his guidance and all the beautiful lessons I've learned from knowing him.

Nancy's Story

It was 1994, and I was working as a nurse case manager for an insurance company. One of my clients was a lovely lady in her mid forties by the name of Nancy. She had a degenerative neurological illness due to a reaction to breast implants and was now paralyzed from her chest down.

I would visit her often to assess her medical needs, as she was quickly deteriorating. Her family very much wanted to keep her at home. She was still very alert. She frequently wanted to discuss spirituality and healing. On this particular day, she was having a lot of pain and difficulty breathing. She asked me if I knew anything about Reiki (healing with channeled energy). I told her that I had been taught Reiki but was very new to it. She asked me if I could do it anyway to see if it would help. I did this, and on further visits (separate from my case management visits), I would bring my Reiki teacher along, and we would both do the treatment. She seemed to relax during the therapy and said she rested better and had less pain for several days following each treatment.

After the treatments, we would visit, and we soon became good friends.

I had visited with Nancy early in the week. Her condition was unchanged, and she was looking forward to a visit from her children. The rest of the week was very busy, and I hadn't spoken with her again. On Friday, I went out of town with my husband for the weekend. We were both very tired and had fallen asleep at about 9:30 p.m.

I soon awoke feeling another presence in the room. I felt very sad and began crying. My husband awoke and asked me what was wrong.

He asked if I had been asleep yet, as it was only 10:10 p.m. I told him that I had fallen asleep but had woken, feeling that Nancy had come to visit and that I was saying good-bye to a very dear friend. After a little while, I went back to sleep.

On Sunday, when I returned home, there was a message from the hospice for me, saying that they thought that I would want to know that Nancy had died on Friday evening at 10:10 p.m.

I will always remember her as a very brave, beautiful, loving lady and feel blessed for having her in my life that short time. And I'll always be grateful that she came to say 'good-bye, see you later' to me.

Angels

Make
yourself
familiar with
the angels,
and behold
them frequently
in spirit;
for without
being seen,
they are present
with you.

—St. Francis de Sales

Wedding Story

I was now in my midforties and had moved to Scotland to marry a wonderful man. I had thought that I would be continuing my HIV work over there but found myself working again in pediatrics. This was great, as I had always loved working with and caring for children. At this time, I was a nursing manager at the Children's Hospital in Edinburgh.

One of my staff came to me on this day and asked if we could go for a cup of coffee. She said that we needed to have a talk, and she appeared quite excited. She was a nurse specialist and cared for children diagnosed with cancer. She explained to me that she had been depressed lately because recently there had been so many children who she was very close to, who had died. She then said, 'You won't believe this, but I was so down that I actually went to see a spiritual medium a friend had recommended'. She felt this medium was authentic, as she had been very specific about several of the children to whom she was closest. She was surprised, as this lady had no idea what she did for a living, saying that one girl was now happy in heaven, and she saw her running very fast in her new tennis shoes. This patient had been on the school's track team and had asked to be buried in her tennis shoes! She then said that the reason she was telling me all of this was that this medium knew of me and that she had something that she must tell me.

In April, my husband and I had been married in a civil ceremony in Edinburgh, followed by a lovely party with our friends and family. It was now May, and we were getting ready to travel back to the States for a spiritual marriage blessing and to celebrate with our American friends. Very skeptically, I went to see this medium before making our trip. As I sat down, she immediately began to tell me of an upcoming celebration and that everyone was very happy. She said that she saw me and a man standing as if in an arch. However, the arch was made up of many little angels, children I knew who had died. They were surrounding us and celebrating with us. She then started naming them and telling me what disease or disorder had caused them to make such early transitions. I realized that they had been children I had been blessed to care for during my many years of nursing. She said that they were all very happy for me and very grateful for my care and were sending much love. She proceeded to tell me that they would find a way of letting me know they were with us on this special day.

A few weeks later, this blessing was taking place on top of a mountain in a beautiful gazebo at sunset. It all seemed very magical. After the blessing, our minister had us turn to face our friends and family. As he was preparing to announce us as man and wife, he paused. He then said that he felt compelled to say something else first. He said, 'You probably know that I'm not really into this "angel thing" that seems to be so popular right now. However, I feel compelled to say that not only are all of your friends and family happy for you and celebrating this wonderful day but that the angels are also here celebrating with you!'

What a wonderful way to end this special ceremony.

In the next room

Death is nothing at all:

I have only slipped away into the next room.

I am I and you are you;

Whatever we were to each other that we are still.

Call me by my old familiar name.

Speak to me in the easy way you always used.

Put no difference in your tone;

Wear no forced air or solemnity or sorrow.

Laugh as we always laughed at the little jokes we shared together.

Play, smile, think of me, pray for me.

Why should I be out of mind because I'm out of sight?

I am but waiting for you, for an interval, somewhere very near,

Just around the corner.

All is well.

—Canon Henry Scott Holland (1847-1918), England

Mom's Story

My husband and I had just returned to Scotland from the United States and were in the process of moving into our new home. While in the States, we had enjoyed the best visit for a very long time with my mother. Although she was eighty-three and had been very ill with chronic kidney problems for a long time, she had been determined to enjoy our visit. While having lunch at the art museum she had become very serious and asked me why I thought she was still here. My father had died over thirty years ago, and she had lost both of her sons over the last five years. I wasn't sure how to answer but stated that I believed we were all here to learn forgiveness and unconditional love. With this, she seemed slightly taken back. She replied, 'Forgiveness? Everyone?' 'Yes, Mom'. 'For everything?' 'Yes, Mom'. 'Oh hell, I'll be here 'til I'm 150!' At this, we had a good laugh.

Mom had previously had two near-death experiences over the last few years and was adamant that she had seen her angel. She recalled that two years previously, she had 'died'. She recalled watching everyone work on resuscitating her, all except one person. This person, who she thought was a nurse, just stood by her bed, all in white, smiling at her. After what seemed like a few minutes to her, she looked down and realized that this 'nurse' was floating, not touching the floor. She said that she then felt great peace and wanted to leave. She recalled being very upset when this being who she now believed to be an angel, told her that she wasn't finished yet and that she must go back. After this episode, I remember her being quite irritated for several weeks that she was still here. She said that it had been such a peaceful experience, and she was really looking forward to going back. She was really tired of the constant pain and inactivity.

It was now July 4, We had been back in Scotland a week and were in the middle of moving house. The phone rang, and it was the rehabilitation centre in Indiana calling to say that my mom was slipping into a coma. She had refused any interventions, and they were calling me to get permission for treatment. I told them that they were to honor my mother's wishes and that I was on my way. I immediately called my oldest son, Tony. We were both concerned that my younger son, who was very close to his grandmother, was camping in Montana; and we had no way to contact him. Tony and I made our flight arrangements. Teri, my daughter, was also making arrangements for her children so she could come as soon as possible. Tony asked what we should do about Todd, his brother. I told him that the only thing I knew to do was to send a Reiki healing to Todd in hopes he would receive it and call home. The next day, when I arrived at the rehab centre, Tony was there to meet me. The first thing he said was, 'Mom, I'll never doubt your Reiki again!' He proceeded to tell me that when he arrived, he had asked for his grandmother's room. The nurse gave him the number and stated that her grandson was already with her. My son told her that that was impossible, as he was her grandson and her other grandson was in Montana. He hurried down to his grandmother's room to find his brother, Todd, reading a book about angels to his grandmother. Todd said that something had woken him in the middle of the night. He knew he needed to come home. He immediately got into the car and drove for the next day and a half. When he got to Indy, instead of going to his home, he went directly to his grandmother.

For the next couple of days, we took shifts as my mother lay in a coma. On this morning, I was alone with her. I did a Reiki healing for her and then sat and talked with her. I told her that all of us were fine and that she could go when she was ready. I reminded her about her angel and about the white light. I then said, 'Mom, let the boys (this is how she always referred to my brothers) help you find the angels'. As I said this, I felt my father standing behind her, so I told her to remember that Dad would also be there to give her support. A few minutes later, a nurse came in to check her vital signs. She said they were very stable and that this may go on for a while. As she left the room, the phone rang. As I answered it, I looked down at my mother. She quietly and effortlessly breathed in and then didn't breathe out. It was as if she just floated away. I kissed her forehead and told her to 'go fly with the angels'.

My three children, her grandchildren, insisted on making all the arrangements for the funeral and even reading the prayers. The day felt full of love and very peaceful.

Two weeks later, when I returned to Scotland, a friend, Angela, called and asked if we could have lunch, as she was having some difficulties with her son. I told her that my mother had died but that I was fine and would give her the details when I saw her. Angela is a well-known spiritual medium.

As we sat down for lunch, Angela started to tell me that she was to do a reading for me. I responded, 'No, this lunch is time for you. I'm really fine'. She answered that my mother was very anxious to talk to me and that she would have no peace until she gave me my mother's messages. She then proceeded to say, 'Your mother says, "Tell Mary Ellen that I found the angels! The boys were helping me all along the way. Tell her also that the tunnel isn't as dark as she thinks it is, and you get help all along the way. Also tell her that when I got here, I turned to see what I had come through, and it had disappeared. Instead her father was standing behind me. Oh, and tell her that they're letting me mind the babies. She'll understand in time."' With this, I told Angela what had happened and what my last words were to my mother. It was so reassuring to know that my mother was safe with her loved ones. However, I couldn't make any sense of the part about minding the babies. My mother, Mary, had always loved babies, but I couldn't see the relevance.

About six months later, I was again in Indiana visiting my son. We had made arrangements to have lunch with some of my old friends. For some reason, I felt I needed to share this story with them. As I finished, I noticed that one of my dearest friends was crying. She has two children, four and six years of age. She proceeded to tell me that since her last child, she had lost two children by miscarriage.

She is very private and, until now, hadn't told anyone about this. She said that she had been pregnant with the fourth child at my mother's funeral and had lost it about a week later. When this happened, she was so grief-stricken that she hadn't known what to do. She wanted to find a way to take care of these two little ones. She then remembered how much Mary had loved children and had asked her to please take care of her babies. Now she felt she could be at peace knowing where her babies were and that Grandma Mary was watching over them.

Healing Hands

Dear God, let my hands

Be always hands of healing

Through which your life

May radiate to lessen pain,

To bring a renewal of peace and healing wherever needed.

Dear God, let my hands

Bring through their touch

Some essence of your love

Flowing through them

To bring comfort and joy.

I offer my hands as a channel;

Use them as your healing tools

—Elizabeth Searle Lamb

Elma's Story

I refer to Reiki in several of my earlier stories. It is a method of channeling healing energy to a person or a situation. People speak of this as acting as a conduit or 'electrical cord' for God's energy or universal energy.

For several years after receiving Reiki, and then learning it, I only used it on myself or my family. However, about ten years ago, I began to see Reiki clients and, quickly thereafter, started to teach it. It has become a very special part of my everyday life.

Sometimes, when doing a Reiki treatment, I will receive a word or image. I've come to understand that whatever I receive is for my client and that I have a responsibility to share this with them when I have finished the treatment. Often, what I get seems a little crazy to me, and I will worry that they will think that I have 'lost it'. However, I know that what they think of me is not important. What is important is that I get my ego out of the way and be totally honest with each client. In order that I remain a clear channel, I don't ask questions of my new clients until after the treatment. I welcome them, explain the Reiki treatment, make them as comfortable as possible, and begin.

During the first year of my practice, one of my clients was a lovely woman in her thirties by the name of Elma. She appeared very happy, friendly, and excited about receiving her first Reiki treatment. She had been referred to me by another client.

I closed my eyes as I began the treatment, and I immediately saw a little robin with a twig in its mouth fly up to her and kiss her on the check. My first thought was, *How am I going to tell her this?* The rest of the treatment was very uneventful, except for feeling a lot of energy flowing through me. But as I was coming to the end of the treatment, I saw a heart-shaped box of chocolates being placed over her heart. Now I knew she would think I was daft!

After the treatment, as we were sitting together, I told her what I had experienced about the robin. She began laughing and crying all at the same time. I sat there in confusion for a few minutes. When she stopped crying, she explained that she had recently lost her husband in an accident and that his name was Robin!

When I then told her of the box of chocolates, she began laughing and crying again! It seems that she and Robin had a longtime joke. He wasn't very good about picking out gifts for her. She would always have to show him what she would like as a present. The only time he had given her a present he chose on his own was when he gave her a heart-shaped box of chocolates. Since that time, he had always said that she would know when a gift was from him because it would be a heart-shaped box of chocolates!

She then began to explain to me the reason that she had come for a Reiki session. Since Robin's death almost a year prior, she had felt that he was still with her.

She believed that he had gone on to the world of spirit but that they still had much work to do together. Many of her friends had discouraged her, saying that it was just her grief and that she had to let him go. She didn't believe this and wanted confirmation that she was on the right path.

Over the years, Elma has gone on to become a wonderful healer and psychic artist, becoming certified in many complementary therapies. She now teaches many of these therapies and acts as a consultant to organizations like the Foster Parent Association.

Two worlds

Though I am gone from this earthly life

My spirit is around you ever watchful and protective

Remember the happy times not the sad

Have no regrets of things unsaid or done

Watch the light of the stars dance on the waterfall

Where our two worlds meet

Please remember me

—Elma Melville (of Elma's Story)

Jane's Story

Jane had been referred to me by a mutual friend. I knew that she had lost her teenage daughter in an accident and was finding each day a struggle.

When she came for her Reiki session, I explained to her what she might expect. I always ask people to feel at ease with any emotions that might come up during the treatment. And I explain that they are free to ask questions or ask me to stop the session at any time.

I thought there might be many tears during this session, and there were some. But there was also a very calm smile on Jane's face throughout the treatment.

You might understand the shock I had when, halfway through the treatment, I 'saw' lemons being sent to her. Yes, she was being showered with lemons! I felt really uncomfortable about sharing this with Jane. She had come to me in such pain, and I was very committed to helping her find some comfort.

This is how the entire session went. At times, Jane lay quietly with a gentle smile on her face. And more often, there were quiet tears. The session was very peaceful. But off and on throughout the entire treatment, there were *lemons*! She was being showered with lemons. How could I tell her she'd been showered with lemons?

I spent the rest of the session asking for guidance, knowing I must share this no matter what she thought of me. As with Elma, when I shared with Jane what I had experienced, she began laughing and crying.

She proceeded to tell me that besides losing her daughter about two years ago, she had recently lost her mother. Her mother had been her best friend and had been there to help her deal with her grief. But when her mother died, she was not only grieving her mother's loss but also the loss of her support in dealing with her daughter's death.

She then started laughing again and told me that she had felt her mother's presence throughout the treatment. This was helping her to feel that her mother was still with her and that she could still count on her support. This was confirmed by me when I told her of the lemons.

You see, her mother thought that lemons could heal anything. Since she was a little girl, the first thing her mother did when Jane was sick or feeling down was to give her lemons! Her mom insisted that lemons could cure anything and everything.

Another major lesson for me in accepting 'what is' without judgment.

No Fear To Die

Teach me your mood, O patient stars,

Who climb each night the ancient sky,

Leaving on space, no shade, no scars,

No trace of age, no fear to die.

—Ralph Waldo Emerson (1803-1882), USA

Joy and Blessings

Whenever there is a problem

Repeat over and over:

'All is well.

Everything is working out

For the highest good.

Out of this situation

Only good will come.

I am safe!'

—Louise L. Hay

Intuition

This is the first time that I remember following my intuition so clearly with regards to using Reiki.

My husband and I were in the process of moving house in Scotland. We were only moving a few miles down the road, so we had been making a number of trips back and forth with household items. It was a Saturday morning just before noon. We were getting ready to go to the car to make yet another trip.

As we were getting ready to leave the house, I suddenly felt a need to stop and ask my husband if he would sit down so I could channel some Reiki for him. He wondered what was wrong with me but agreed to do so. I felt drawn to Reiki his legs, especially his right leg. I assumed that he had been working very hard and just needed some energy.

We then left for the old house with him driving. He had only driven about two miles when we came to an intersection. He had the green light, so we proceeded through the intersection. Suddenly, another car appeared, going very fast, and coming from the other direction. He had the red light, slammed on his brakes, but was unable to stop the car. It was a car full of young people in a hurry to get to a wedding.

The car impacted our car on my husband's side, in the middle of the driver's door, where his right knee was!

The other car was totaled and our car had extensive damage. The entire front had to be rebuilt. However, thankfully, no one was hurt. And even though my husband's knee had been exactly where the impact occurred, he didn't have even a bruise.

I now often use Reiki to put protective energy around myself and my loved ones.

The Healer Within

The natural healing force

Within each one of us

Is the greatest force

In getting well

—Hippocrates

Rory's Story

I had just moved to the Lowcountry of South Carolina with my husband, preparing for his upcoming retirement.

We were immediately blessed with wonderful friends and neighbors, especially one lovely lady who went out of her way to orient me to the area, its history, and its customs. I immediately felt at home here, even though my husband was still traveling with his work a great deal.

One day, while taking a walk with this new friend, she appeared sad. As we talked, she told me that she didn't know what to do about her dog, Rory. Rory was twelve years old and was having problems with her hip. This was making it almost impossible for Rory to walk, and she appeared to be in a great deal of pain. She and her husband were having a dilemma as to what to do. The veterinarian had told them that surgery would be over $2000, and because of Rory's age, she may not survive. He had suggested putting Rory to sleep, but my friend really didn't want to do this if there were any other choices.

After listening for a few minutes, I asked her if she had ever heard of Reiki. She hadn't, so I proceeded to explain that it was one of many effective methods of channeling healing energy. My friend was very interested and asked me if I could do a treatment with Rory.

When we returned to her house, we went to find Rory. I sat on the ground close to Rory quietly until she seemed comfortable with me. I moved close and placed my hands on her hips. After a couple of minutes, Rory seemed to relax. We sat there together while the energy flowed for about fifteen minutes. At that point, Rory seemed to begin to get restless, so I stopped the Reiki session.

For the following few weeks I would go over to visit Rory every couple of days. I would sit down on the lawn, and each time, she would come over to me and turn so that she was placing her hips on my lap as she sat down. I would begin the Reiki session, and we would sit quietly together.

Every time, just as I begin to notice the heat or tingling in my hands dissipating, Rory would stand up and walk away. She always knew when her treatment was over.

That was four and a half years ago. Rory, thankfully, is still with us. She and my friend take long daily walks together, and I often look out my window to see her, across the street, chasing the squirrels.

We are what we think

All that we are arises with our thoughts.

With our thoughts

We make the world.

—Buddha

Matthew's Story

While living in Scotland, I was blessed with many experiences of working with children using alternative therapies. At the Edinburgh Children's Hospital, where I worked, there were studies being conducted to see how Reiki and reflexology helped with symptom control for children dealing with cancer; and there was also a very successful study regarding using reflexology for children suffering with severe constipation. Several times, staff at the home for children with complex disabilities asked me to use Reiki for seizure control.

But the situation that stands out most in my mind was a little boy by the name of Jeff and his brother, Matthew.

Jeff's mother had been referred to me by a community nurse. He was four years old and had suffered from severe dermatitis for over two years. He had been to several doctors, and his mother had tried all of their suggestions without any improvement in his skin condition. He was often in pain and agitated from the constant itching and burning. It covered much of his body. Because of this, he also had great difficulty sleeping, which only added to his and his mother's level of frustration.

Out of desperation, the mother had asked this nurse if there was anything else that she might try to help Jeff. The nurse suggested that she might give Reiki a try and gave her my name.

When Jeff and his mother showed up for the Reiki session, they were very anxious. His mother told me that she and her husband were very conservative, didn't know anything about alternative therapies, but were desperate.

I explained as best I could about energy and how we can assist in channeling it for healing. I told Jeff what I would be doing and asked his mother to join us for the Reiki session. She stated that she was concerned because Jeff was hyperactive, and the dermatitis was making him more agitated. I talked with Jeff about what things he liked and what might make him more comfortable during the session. Lying on a table in a quiet room just didn't seem his thing! We agreed that we would sit on the floor, and he would play my Native American drum while I channeled the Reiki. I put my hand over his arm and told him that he might feel cold or heat or tingling, that any of that was just energy working to heal him. I asked his mother to stay with us so that he would feel comfortable.

I was surprised when he would stop drumming for a minute several times to say, 'It's not tingly anymore. You need to move your hand' very matter-of-factly.

At the end of the session, both his mother and I were surprised at how calm he was. All he said about the treatment was, 'Yeah. It felt good'.

We agreed that I would see them again the following week.

When Jeff and his mother came the following week for the treatment, they had his brother, Matthew, with them. Matthew was ten years old and very quiet.

I asked him if he would like to use my computer while we went into the therapy room for Jeff's treatment. He said that he loved computers and would be very happy to do that. I showed him where we would be and told him that he could join us at any time if he had a question or became bored.

Now I must divert to give you some background for what happened next.

One of my nursing managers had come to me a few years prior to this to tell me that she had been to see a well-known clairvoyant. She had never been to any type of psychic before, but her friend kept talking about this man and how wonderful he was. His name was Colin Grant, and he was a great-grandfather, who had been giving readings in his small office just off of the High Street in Edinburgh all of his adult life. He often worked with the local police and was written up in the newspaper from time to time.

She told me that her reading had been very good but that what stayed with her was that he kept referring to her American boss (me). He told her that she would be following the same career path as I, with a chance to manage a large community health program. This has since proved to be true. He told her that he wanted to meet me and that he had a message for me.

Out of curiosity, I made an appointment with him. When I arrived, I was greeted by his lovely wife of sixty-plus years. His reading was very helpful, but I believe that the main purpose of the reading was that we become friends. I truly felt like I had re-met an old, dear friend.

After that, when I was in the city, I would stop by and have a chat and a cup of tea with him and his wife whenever I could. He had never traveled but was fascinated by other countries and cultures. He also had a deep love of nature and loved to collect stones. They were placed very thoughtfully all around his office.

I was blessed to be able to travel to many countries with my husband as a result of his work. I would always try to bring back a stone for Colin and his wife. We often discussed these different places, he and I always agreeing that our favorite place was Hawaii. I had brought him back a special stone from Kauai, which he kept on his desk.

A couple of months before I started to do Reiki treatments for Jeff, my husband and I had been in the States visiting family. While there, Colin kept popping into my mind. My only thought was that I must catch up with him when we returned home to Scotland.

I was really taken aback when we returned home and checked our phone messages. There were several calls to let me know that Colin had died (at his desk while giving a reading) while we were away. There had been a huge write-up and tribute to him in the newspaper, and several people who knew we were good friends wanted to let me know about his passing.

I then knew why he kept popping into my mind. I was only sorry that I hadn't been able to say good-bye to this wise, compassionate man.

But I hadn't thought much about it the past few weeks.

Now back to Jeff's Reiki session. Matthew stayed downstairs, and we didn't hear from him until the end of the session. When we went to find him, he had a very perplexed look on his face. He said, 'This has never happened to me before. When I went onto the computer, it was as if someone else was with me. I *had* to print this card for you. I don't know why and I don't know what it means'. The card was of a rainbow in Hawaii, and across the top of the rainbow was printed 'See you on the other side'.

I explained about Colin and we all stood there feeling stunned. But Matthew also seemed quite happy that he wasn't going crazy and that it had great meaning to me. He asked if you had to be sick to have a Reiki treatment. I told him that it was all about receiving energy and that we can all benefit from that. So we scheduled him for a Reiki session the following week.

When Matthew arrived for his session, he seemed very quiet, not knowing what he would experience. I told him that we could do what we did for his brother with the drumming or art during the session if that would help him to relax. He wanted to know what the adults did. I told him that they usually lay on the table with the lights low and some peaceful music to relax. He was very clear that he wanted to be treated like the adults.

He lay quietly for the first part of the treatment. But about halfway through, he opened his eyes and smiled at me, saying, 'If this is what heaven is like, I can't wait to get there!'

Matthew had a few more treatments and then asked if he could take the Reiki classes. His mother also wanted to take the classes, as Jeff's skin condition was slowly improving. They took both Reiki I and II.

About this time, I began having Reiki get-togethers monthly at my house. These were open to anyone, who had taken any level of Reiki. Matthew not only came whenever possible but would also offer to open the meeting by leading us in amazing angel meditations. This quickly became the favorite part of our meetings for the rest of the practitioners.

Jeff continued to improve. His mother told me that she now would lay with him at night and send Reiki to him, which enabled him to quickly go to sleep and sleep well throughout the night.

Consciousness and Healing

Complete Health

And

Awakening

Are really the same.

—Tarthang Tulku

Healing As Our Birthright

We attend in silence and in joy.

This is the day when healing comes to us.

This is the day when separation ends,

And we remember Who we really are.

—Quote from 'A Course in Miracles'

My Personal Angel

When living in Scotland, we were blessed with a lovely old house, parts of it more than two hundred years old. When we first moved into our home in the summer of 1996, I tried to find more information about the house but had little success. So I decided to turn it over to Spirit. If we were suppose to know about the house, the information would be presented to me at the right time. I then put it out of my mind and got on with the much-needed renovations.

I had pretty much forgotten about this issue when, at Christmas time, we received a holiday card that was addressed 'To the new owners of Harvieston Tollhouse'. As I opened it, I received a wonderful surprise. Inside it simply said, 'Hi, my name is Margaret and I was born in the Tollhouse, as was my father. Most of my family has grown up there. We hope you are very happy there, as we were. If you would like more information about the house please feel free to contact me at____'.

I couldn't get to the phone fast enough! I immediately invited this lovely lady to coffee. She came the following week, bringing photos of the house and her family. The photos were of her grandparents, who were the first ones to live in the house, of her parents, siblings, children, and grandchildren. It was a gold mine of information about this lovely place. It was amazing to see that her parents had driven a red MG, just as we now did, and parked it in the same place as we did. She told me about how she remembered her grandparents planting the plum trees in our back garden, the ones where I had just picked plums from and tried my first attempt at plum jam.

Because I was so excited about all of this information, she left the photos with me to copy. I assembled a few of these photos, showing a history of the house, framed them, and hung them in the entryway to our home. I made a pledge to Grandpa that I knew it would always really be his home, and I would take very good care of it.

Although we were out in the country, surrounded on three sides by sprawling farmland, I always felt very safe. My husband traveled a lot, so I was often on my own. If I ever felt a little lonely, I would go into the living room at the front of the house, which was the oldest part, sit in front of the fireplace, and feel very safe and cozy. Margaret and the rest of her previous family had become very good friends. On one occasion, I mentioned this to Margaret, and she told me that this room was also the favorite of her father and grandfather.

We had been living in this home for about five years when something really unusual happened. It was a Thursday night and I had been asleep for several hours. My husband was away on business. At 2:00 a.m., I was awakened by thoughts going through my head, saying, 'Wake up, you are going to be robbed!' I never worried about such a thing, so this felt very foreign to me. I sat up in bed to make sure I was awake and not just having a bad dream.

But the thoughts continued 'Do you know the number to call for emergencies? Keep your cell phone with you and the house phone close at hand. If you are here when they come, where will you hide? If you come home and discover evidence of someone being in the house, stay outside and phone the police'. Someone was preparing me to handle this possible situation. This was so real that I went downstairs and looked up all the emergency numbers. It was also so real that I couldn't go back to sleep, so I sat on the couch, looking out the front window for hours.

I finally fell asleep on the couch and woke up at about 7:00 a.m. My first thought was, 'Well, I guess that was just a bad dream'. I got ready and went to work.

It was a very busy day, and I pretty much forgot about the previous night's activities.

After work, I went out with some friends for dinner and a play. I was driving home around midnight and made a wrong turn. This took me about ten minutes out of my way. But I do believe things happen for a reason, and I remember thinking, 'Oh well, maybe I'm avoiding an accident'. This was the way I drove home every evening, so making a wrong turn was highly unusual.

When I parked in my driveway and walked up to the door, I saw mud footprints across the entryway. About this time, I heard the back door slam.

I stayed outside and phoned the police.

In about five minutes, the police were there. They went into the house and verified that the burglar had indeed left through the back door. I then went through the house with the police, tracing his steps and checking for missing items and damage. It was easy to trace his activities because he had come through a very muddy field and left prints throughout the house. The only damage he had done was a broken window in the room where he had entered. This room had been set up as a meditation room. It was obvious that he was trying not to damage anything. He had carefully turned figurines and vases on their side so as not to break them before opening furniture draws.

When we went into my bedroom, we could see two footprints in front of my window, overlooking the driveway. It was obvious that he had been watching me as I pulled into the driveway.

The officer then said, 'You know, if you had been ten minutes earlier, he would have been at the other end of the house. The way this house is constructed, he would have had to come face-to-face with you in order to get out!'

Boy, was I glad that I had made that wrong turn!

He had taken some wine and a traveler's check, but that was about all. The police called someone to board up my window until morning and then, after ensuring that I was okay, left. They assured me that they would have someone back first thing in the morning.

As they drove out of the driveway, I heard, 'You're safe now. It's over'. The words came to me just as they had the night before when woken from my sleep. I went to bed and slept soundly.

The next morning, when again talking with the police, I told them that I felt that this person was not a bad person, just desperate. I asked them to tell this person, when they caught them, that if they wanted help, my husband and I would like to help in any way we could. They agreed that this was a desperate person, probably a drug addict.

A few weeks later, another policeman showed up at my door, saying he wanted to ask me some questions about the burglary. He informed me that they had arrested someone, and he had confessed to the burglary.

He then asked if he could see the room where this man had broken into. I answered, 'Of course, but the room has been cleaned a long time ago and put back to normal'. He proceeded to tell me that he only wanted to see the room out of interest.

Apparently, the burglar, at the time of his arrest, freely admitted to robbing my home, along with four other homes in the neighborhood. 'He didn't seem concerned about his arrest', the policeman informed me, 'he only wanted to tell me about this room and about your home. He told me that I had to come and see this room'.

The policeman then told me that the man was a single parent with a serious drug problem, who had been arrested several times for the same kind of thing. His little boy was often left to wander the streets and care for himself.

The burglar had requested treatment. He had previously been offered treatment but had always refused it.

Several years later, I was told that this man is now doing much better and caring well for his little boy. I'll always believe that the angels who watched over that house had, in some way, helped this man to see that there was a better way to live.

The Beauty of the Universe

What is it that you see today

When you look up close or far away,

Do you see the beauty of the universe?

When you walk along the street

And smile at the friends you meet,

Do you see the beauty of the universe?

As you hear the birds that sing

And fill with all the joy they bring,

Do you see the beauty of the universe?

Looking up into the sky

As clouds go gently floating by,

Do you see the beauty of the universe?

When you look into your heart

And find the strength to do your part,

Do you see the beauty of the universe?

You need not look outside at all

For God gives everyone their call

To be the beauty of the universe.

—Keith W. Roessing

Thank you to all those who have inspired me to write this book
and allowed me to share their stories.
You truly are 'the beauty of the universe'!

Edwards Brothers,Inc!
Thorofare, NJ 08086
28 October, 2010
BA2010302